Unit 1

1a

Helga Schmidt – 12
Grünberg Hauptschule, Neustadt

John Brown – 11
Hill School, Liverpool

What's your name?
Helga Schmidt.

What's your name?
John Brown

What's your name?
Daniela Pfeuffer

Are you English?
No, I'm not. I'm German.

Are you German?
Yes, I'm.

Are you English?
No, I'm not. I'm German.

How old are you?
I'm twelve.

How old are you?
I'm eleven

How old are you?
I'm ten.

Are you at Hill School?
No, I'm not. I'm a pupil at Grünberg Hauptschule.

Are you at Grünberg Hauptschule?
No, I'm not. I'm a pupil at Hill School

Are you at Hill School?
No, I'm not. I'm a pupil at Hauptschool.

möglicher Einsatzort nach 1a, S. 7

1b

HELGA SCHMIDT
I'm Helga Schmidt. I'm not English. I'm German. I'm twelve. I'm a pupil at Grünberg Hauptschule in Neustadt.

JOHN BROWN
I'm John Brown. I'm English. I'm not German. I'm eleven. I'm a pupil at Hill School in Liverpool.

_Daniela Pfeuffer
I'm Daniela Pfeuffer. I'm not English. I'm German. I'm ten. I'm a pupil at Hauptschool in Arnstein_

1a, S. 7

2

Yes, I am. / No, I'm not.

1. Are you German? _Yes, I am._
2. Are you a teacher? _No, I'm not._
3. Are you in Class 1F? _No, I'm not._
4. Are you a pupil? _Yes, I am._
5. Are you in Class 5? _Yes, I am._
6. Are you English? _No, I'm not._

1a, S. 7

3 The Webbs

 1. Eric  2. Carol  3. Mr Webb  4. Mrs Webb  5. Susan  6. Terry

1. **His** name is Eric Webb.
2. **Her** name is Carol Webb.
3. His name is Mr Webb.
4. Her name is Mrs Webb.
5. Her name is Susan Webb.
6. His name is Terry Webb.

1b, S. 8

4

a. 1. Mr Webb is **tall and dark.**
2. Mrs Webb is **small and** fair.
3. Terry Webb is tall and fair.
4. Carol Webb is tall and dark.
5. Eric Webb is small and dark.
6. Susan Webb is small and fair.

b. 1. Is Terry dark? – **No, he isn't. He's fair.**
2. Is Carol small? – **No, she isn't. She's tall.**
3. Is Mr Webb fair? – No, he isn't. He's dark.
4. Is Susan tall? – No, she isn't. She's small.
5. Is Mrs Webb dark? – No, she isn't. She's fair.
6. Is Eric fair? – No, he isn't. He's dark.

1b, S. 8

5

My friend is Harry. He's English. He's small and fair. Harry is eleven and he's a pupil at Hill School, too. He's in Class 1B. His teacher is Mr Green. Mr Green is tall and dark.

Tim Lee 1F.

My friend is Gillian. She's German. She's tall and fair. Gillian is eleven and she's a pupil at Hauptschool too. She's in Class 5.b. Her teacher is Mrs Rolek. Mrs Rolek is tall and dark. Daniela Pfeuffer 5 b

1b, S. 8

6a English – German?

1. Here are _English schools._   2. Here are _German_ t_eachers_

3. Here are _English_ p_upils_   4. Here are _German_ g_irls_   5. _Here are English_ b_oys_

6b

1. The schools **aren't** German.   They**'re** English.
2. The teachers **aren't** English.   They**'re** _German._
3. The pupils _aren't German_   They're _English._
4. The girls _aren't English._   _They're German._
5. The boys _aren't German_   _They're English_

7 You and your friend

Your names: _Diana Pfeiffer_   _Yvonne Mützel_

Yes, we are. / No, we aren't.

1. Are you 14? _No, we aren't._   4. Are you English? _No, we aren't._
2. Are you at the same school? _Yes, we are_   5. Are you in the same class? _No, we aren't._
3. Are you 9? _No, we aren't._   6. Are you German? _Yes, we are._

8

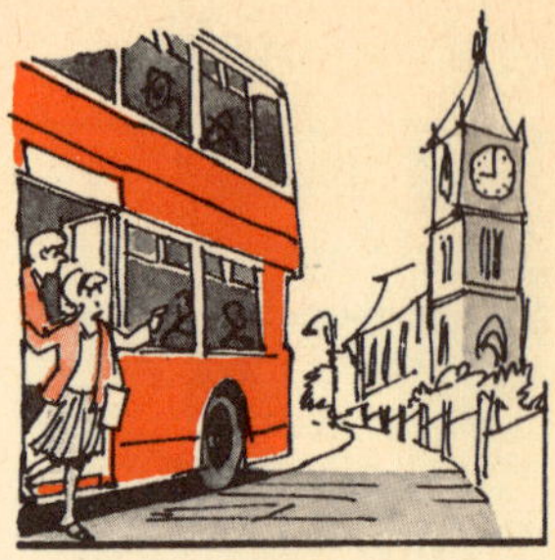

Pete and Pam are English. ☒ / German. ☐ / dark. ☐

They're teachers. ☐ / pupils. ☒ / girls. ☐

They're boys. ☐ / teachers. ☐ / friends. ☒

"We're German." ☐ / dark." ☐ / late." ☒

They're in the same class. ☒ / tall and dark. ☐ / small. ☐

"Goodbye, Mrs Tap." ☐ / "Good morning, Mrs Tap." ☒ / "Hallo, Mrs Tap." ☐

"You're English." ☐ / late." ☒ / teachers." ☐

"Of course." ☐ / "Goodbye." ☐ / "Sorry." ☒

9

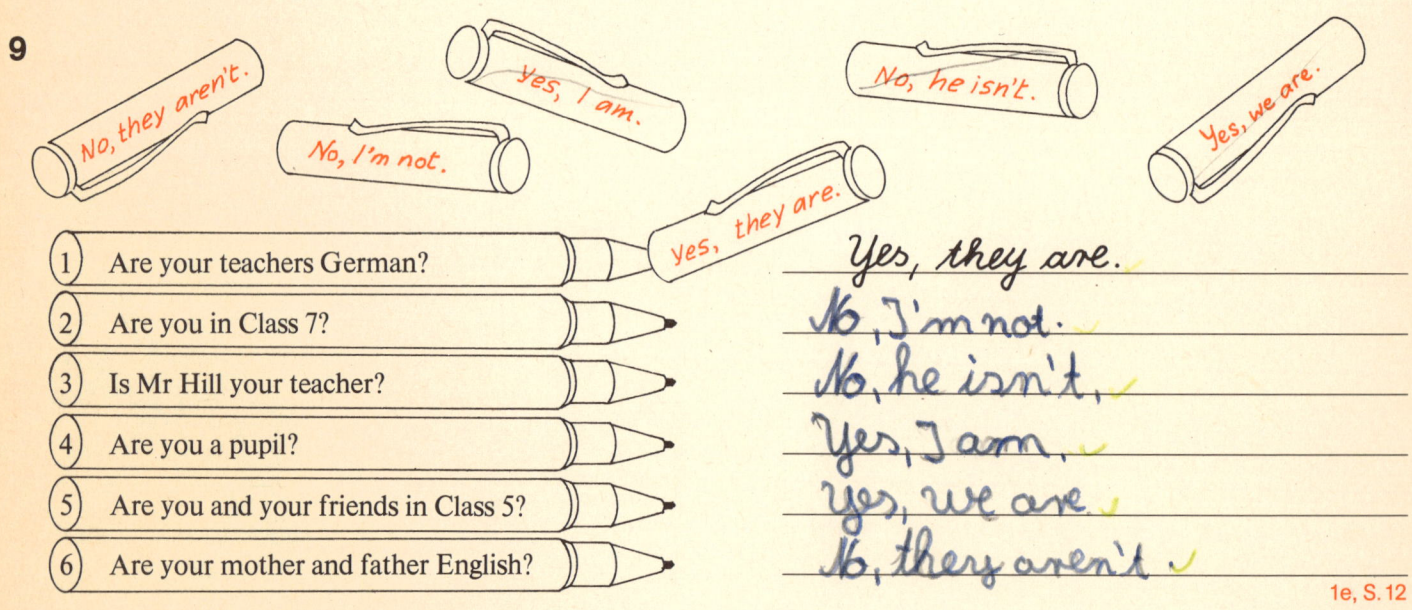

1. Are your teachers German? — Yes, they are.
2. Are you in Class 7? — No, I'm not.
3. Is Mr Hill your teacher? — No, he isn't.
4. Are you a pupil? — Yes, I am.
5. Are you and your friends in Class 5? — Yes, we are.
6. Are your mother and father English? — No, they aren't.

10

1. Mr Hill is a _teacher_.
2. "Good _morning_, Mr Hill."
3. Ann Green is a _girl_.
4. Mr Brown isn't tall. He's _small_.
5. Dave and Ann are in the _same_ class.
6. "What's your _name_?" – "Tony."
7. Alan isn't fair. He's _dark_.

Liverpool is in ⟶

Unit 2

1 Who's that?

Jenny: Who's that?
Peter: My friend.
Her name is Sue.

John: Who's _that_ ?
Jim: My _brother._
His _name is Tony._

Bobby: _Who's that_ ?
Mrs Lee: _My sister._
Her name is Jennie.

Janet: _Who's that_ ?
Mike: _My teacher._
Her name is Miss Lamb.

Kate: _Who's that_ ?
Wendy: _My friend._
His name is Brian.

Mary: _Who's that_ ?
David: _My teacher._
Her name is Mrs Bell.

2a, S. 14

2a Harry's family

1. Joe is Harry's father.
2. _Mary_ is _Harry's mother._
3. _Jane_ is _Harry's sister._
4. _Robert_ is _Harry's brother._

2a, S. 14

2b My family

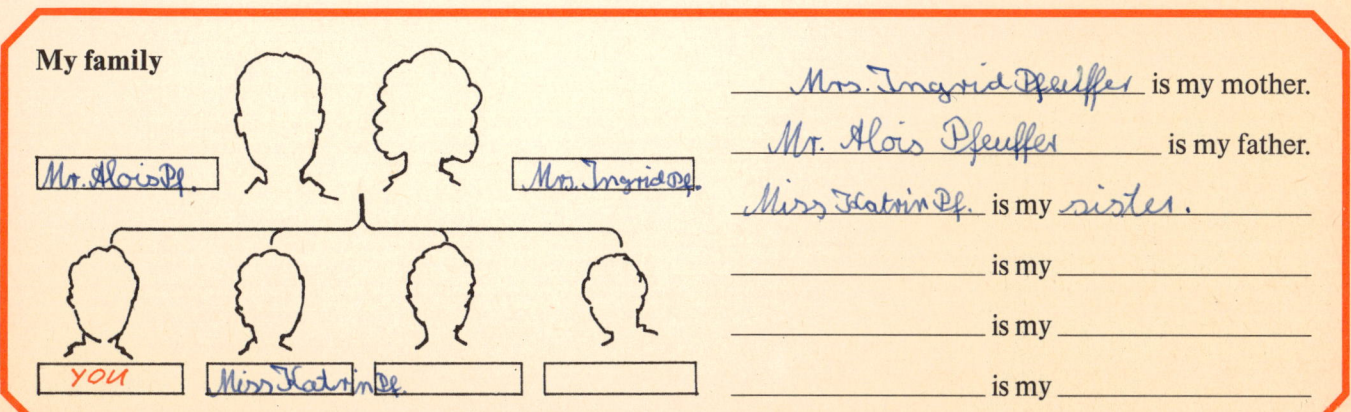

Mrs. Ingrid Pfeiffer is my mother.
Mr. Alois Pfeiffer is my father.
Miss Katrin Pf. is my _sister._
_____ is my _____
_____ is my _____
_____ is my _____

2a, S. 14

5

3  **Brothers and sisters**

Tom: I've got a brother but I haven't got a sister.

 Jane: I've got a sister but I haven't got a brother

 Bob: I've got a sister and a brother.

You: I've got a sister but I haven't got a brother

4

have got / haven't got
1. The Browns **have got** a house.
2. They **have got** a garden.
3. They **haven't got** a car.
4. They **haven't got** a garage.

Yes, they have. / No, they haven't.
5. Have the Browns got a garden?
   Yes, they have (a garden.)
6. Have the Browns got a car?
   No, they haven't (a car.)
7. Have the Browns got a garage?
   No, they haven't (a garage.)
8. Have the Browns got a house?
   Yes, they have (a house.)

5 **We have got / We haven't got**
1. We have got a house.
2. We haven't got a flat.
3. We have got a garage.
4. We have got a car.
5. We have got a TV.
6. We have got a balcony.

Yes, we have. / No, we haven't.
1. Have you got a house? Yes, we have.
2. Have you got a flat? No, we haven't.
3. Have you got a garage? Yes, we have
4. Have you got a car? Yes, we have
5. Have you got a TV? Yes, we have.
6. Have you got a balcony? Yes, we have.

6 NAME: David Carter

What have you got?

A dog	✓
A cat	—
A rabbit	—
A record-player	✓
A calculator	—

1. I've got a dog.
2. I haven't got a cat.
3. I haven't got a rabbit.
4. I have got a record-player.
5. I haven't got a calculator.

NAME: Daniela Pfeuffer

What have you got?

A dog	—
A cat	—
A rabbit	—
A record-player	✓
A calculator	✓

And you?

1. I haven't got a dog.
2. I haven't got a cat.
3. I haven't got a rabbit.
4. We have got a record-player.
5. We have got a calculator.

2c, S. 18

7 Have they got…?

a pencil, a felt-tip, a calculator, a pen, a biro, a ruler, a rubber

Pete has got a rubber, a pen, a felt-tip and a calculator _____ in his pencil-case.
He hasn't got a biro, a pencil or a ruler.

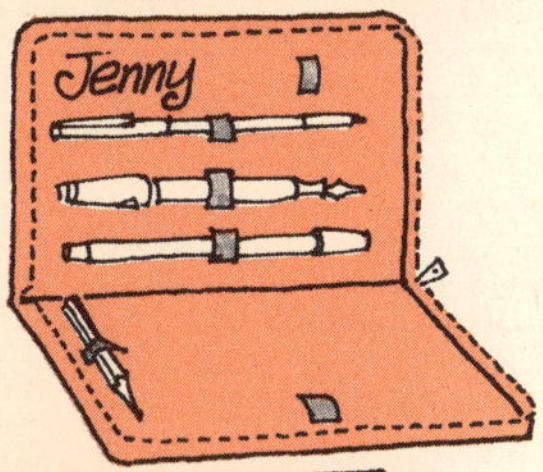

Jenny has got a pencil, a pen, a biro, and a felt-tip _____ in her pencil-case.
She hasn't got a rubber and a calculator

David has got a biro, a pencil, a calculator, and a ruler _____ in his pencil-case.
He hasn't got a rubber, a pen and a felt-tip

I've got a pen, a pencil, a ruler, a felt-tip and a rubber _____ in my pencil-case.

I haven't got a biro and a calculator

2c, S. 19

8

HARDY SCHOOL
Name: Ann Brown — 12
Class: 2F
Sister(s): Sandra — 2
Brother(s): David — 11 [CLASS 1F]

My name is Ann Brown. I'm twelve.
I'm in Class 2F at Hardy School.
I've got a sister — she's two.
I've got a brother — he's eleven.
He's in Class 1F.

HILL SCHOOL
Name: Glen Scott — 11
Class: 1A
Sister(s): Mary — 13 (Class 3A)
Brother(s): Andrew — 9

My name is Glen Scott. I'm eleven. I'm in Class 1A at Hill School.
I've got a sister — she's thirteen.
She is in Class 3A.
I've got a brother — he is nine.

Hauptschool
Name: Daniela Pfeuffer — 10
Class: 5b
Sister(s): Katrin — Class 3b
~~Brother(s):~~

And you?

My name is Daniela Pfeuffer.
I'm ten. I'm in Class 5b.
I've got a sister — she nine.
She is in Class 3b.

2d, S. 20

9

1. What's that?
   It's a calculator.

$100 - 49 + 9 \times 2 - 108 = \ ?$

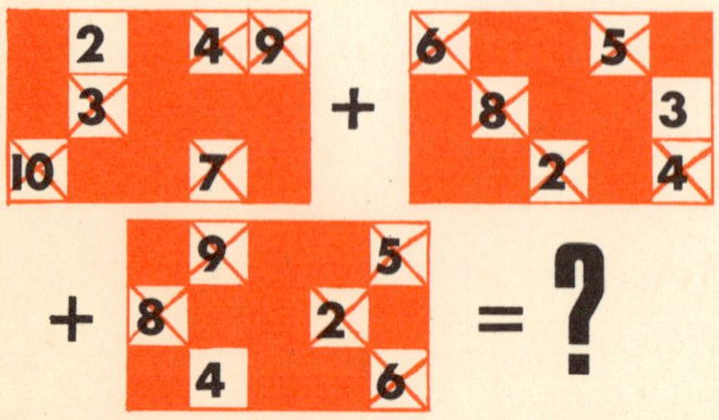

4. How old is Susan?
   She's _twelve_.

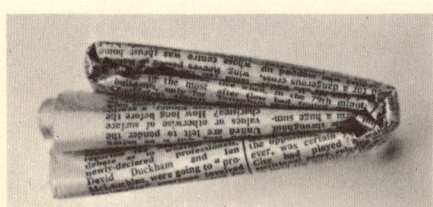

2. What's _that_ ?
   It's a newspaper

5. _How old is_ Ted?
   He's _nine_.

3. _What's that_ ?
   It's a pencil.

6. _How old is_ Mary?
   She's two.

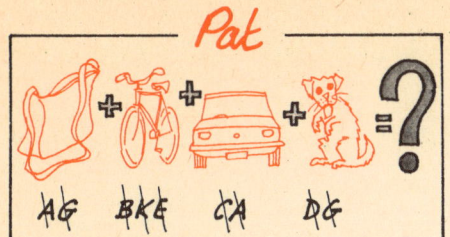

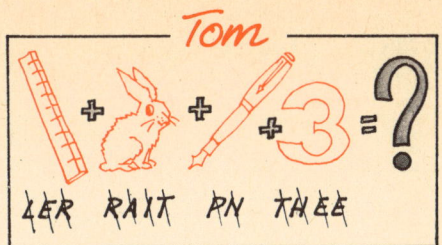

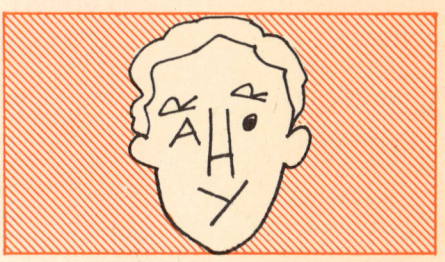

Pat
AG BKE CA DG
Tom
LER RAIT PN THEE
Jim
GIL CALCATOR HOUS GADEN

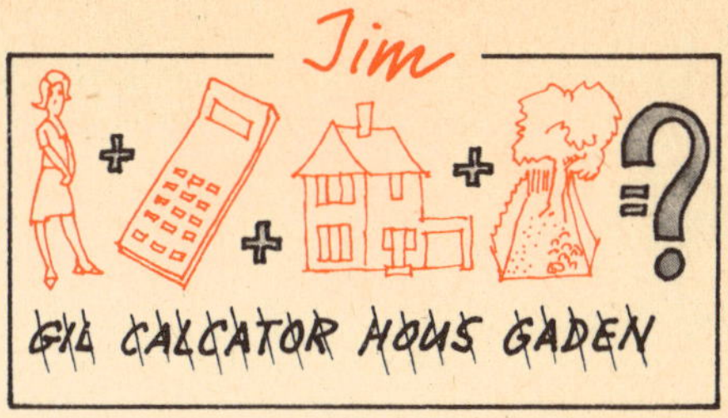

7. What has Pat got?
She has got a biro.

8. What has Tom got?
He has got a rubber.

9. What has Jim got?
He has got a ruler.

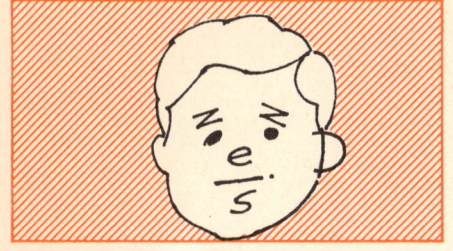

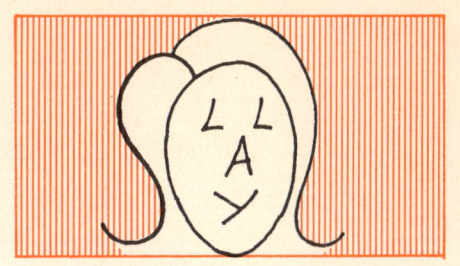

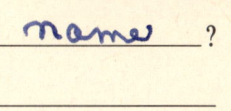

10. What's his name?
Dennis.

11. What's her name?
Sally.

12. What's his name?
Harry.

2e, S. 21

10

t	h	o	r	o	s	t	p	i
h	l	r	c	p	i	z	o	y
i	m	f	d	f	s	j	g	m
r	u	l	e	r	t	i	a	o
t	e	a	c	h	e	r	r	t
e	x	t	a	o	r	o	a	h
e	k	l	m	z	p	h	g	e
n	e	w	s	p	a	p	e	r

1. Father and mother.
2. Mr Hill is Ann Green's teacher.
3. The car is in the garage.
4. I've got a brother and a sister.
5. The TV programmes are in the newspaper
6. We haven't got a house but we've got a flat
7. Eleven and two is thirteen.
8. Pencil, rubber and ruler.

2e, S. 21

11

What has Jim got in his bag?

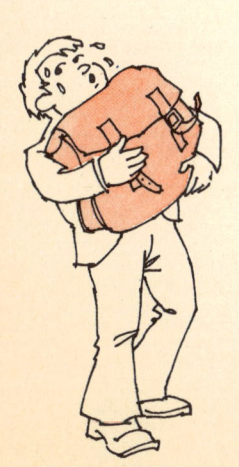

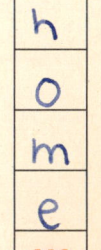

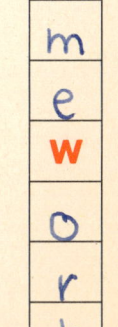

1. house
2. dog
3. magazine
POP
4. pencil

h o m e w o r k

5. twelve
6. biro
7. rabbit
8. bike

2e, S. 21

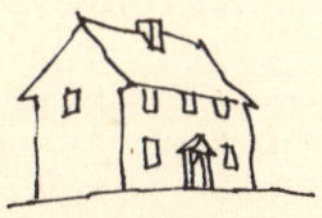

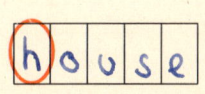

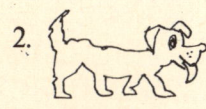

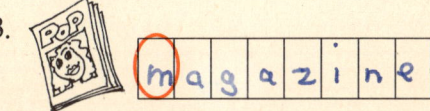

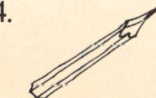

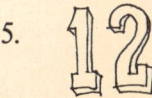

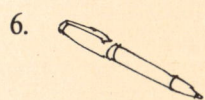

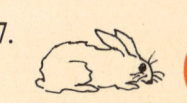

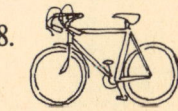

Unit 3

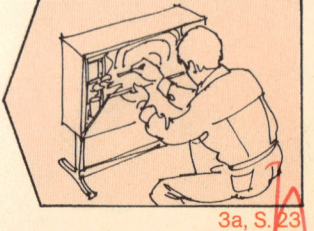

1 buy, clean, go, paint, repair

1. Mr Lane: Buy a newspaper, please.
   Sally Lane is buying a newspaper.

2. Mrs White: Clean your room, please.
   Jack White is cleaning his room.

3. Mrs Potter: Paint the balcony, please.
   Mr Potter is painting the balcony.

4. Mr Smith: Repair the car, please.
   Mr Brown is repairing the car.

5. Mrs Low: Go to the shops, please.
   Mary Low is going to the shops.

6. Mrs Mark: Paint the house, please.
   Mr Evans is painting the house.

7. Mr Rice: Clean the car, please.
   Dave Rice is cleaning the car.

8. Mr Day: Repair the TV, please.
   Mr Cabel is repairing the TV.

2

(buying)
He _isn't buying_ a newspaper.

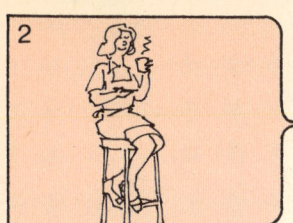
(cleaning)
She _isn't cleaning_ Jack's room.

(painting)
She _isn't painting_ the balcony. ✓

(repairing)
He _isn't repairing_ his car. ✓

(going)
She _isn't going_ to the shops. ✓

(painting)
She _isn't painting_ her house. ✓

(cleaning)
He _isn't cleaning_ his car. ✓

(repairing)
He _isn't repairing_ his TV. ✓

3a, S. 24

3

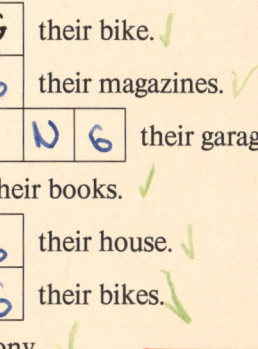

1. Jack and Tom are **RIDING** their bike. ✓
2. Sue and Jill are **READING** their magazines. ✓
3. Mr and Mrs Lee are **PAINTING** their garage. ✓
4. Jane and Mike are **READING** their books. ✓
5. Sam and Mr Bell are **PAINTING** their house. ✓
6. Johnny and Susie are **RIDING** their bikes. ✓
7. The Sims are **CLEANING** their balcony. ✓
8. Mr and Mrs Low are **PAINTING** their car. ✓
9. The boys are **RIDING** their bikes. ✓
10. What are David and Peter doing?
    They're **REPAIRING** their bikes. ✓

3a, S. 25

4

5

aren't painting, aren't repairing, aren't cleaning

1. The boys _aren't repairing_ their bikes.
2. The girls _aren't cleaning_ their room.
3. Mr and Mrs Cox _aren't painting_ their room.

6

1. What's Susan doing? — She's repairing her car.
2. What are Dave and Sam doing? — They're painting the garage.
3. What's Derek _doing_? — He's _riding his bike_.
4. What are Jill and Mike _doing_? — They're _watching TV_.
5. What's _Bob doing_? — _He's reading a newspaper_.
6. What are _Mary and Pam doing_? — _They're repairing bikes_.
7. _What's Linda doing_? — _She's going to the shops_.
8. _What's Jean doing_? — _She's cleaning her room_.
9. _What are Ann and Polly doing_? — _They're cleaning the car_.

7

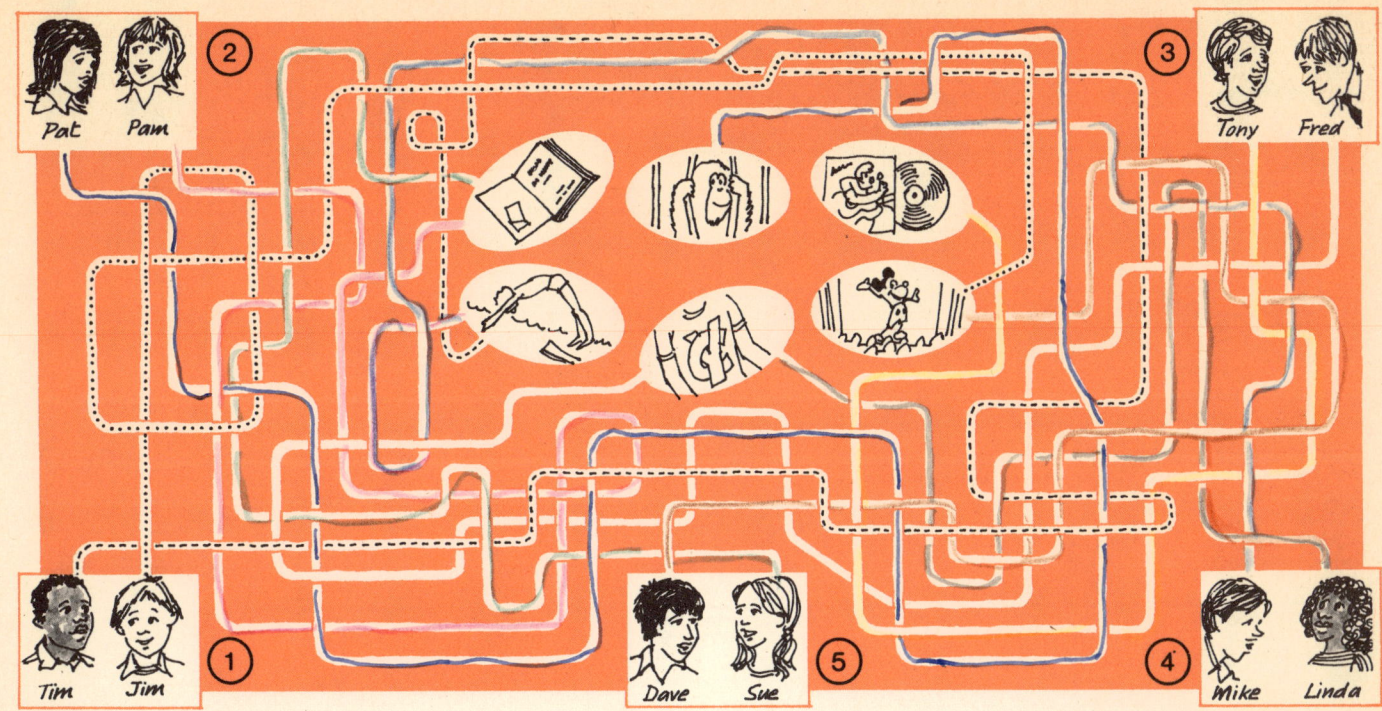

1. Tim: I'm going to the baths.   Are you coming?
   Jim: Sorry, I'm going to the cinema.
2. Pat: I'm *going to the zoo*   Are *you coming*?
   Pam: Sorry, I'm *going to the library.*
3. Tony: *I'm going to the record shop*   *Are you coming*?
   Fred: *Sorry, I'm going to the yoth club.*
4. Mike: *I'm going to the baths.*   *Are you coming*?
   Linda: *Sorry. I'm going to the yoth club.*
5. Dave: *I'm going to the cinema.*   *Are you coming*?
   Sue: *Sorry. I'm going to the library.*

3c, S. 28

8

Tom: Where's Dave?

Mary: He's at the…

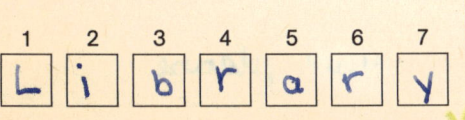
L i b r a r y

 pup [2] ls
 gi [6] l
 balcon [7]
 [4] abbit
 te [5] cher
 [3] oy
 po [1] iceman

3e, S. 30

13

Unit 4

1 What's in the pet shop?

1. There's a _dog in the pet shop._
2. _There's_ a _cat in the pet shop._
3. _There's a hamster in the pet shop_
4. _There's a budgie._
5. There are some _rabbits._
6. _There are_ some _boxes._
7. _There are some cages._
8. _There are some baskets._

4a, S. 32

2 What's in the garage?

1. There's a cage.
2. There are some boxes.
3. _There's a bag._
4. _There are some newspapers._
5. _There's a bike._
6. _There are some baskets._
7. _There's a TV._
8. _There are some cats._

But there isn't a car!

4a, S. 32

3

Can I have your magazine, please?

Can I have your calculator, please?

Can I have your ruler, please?

4

1. Can I _have a new biro_ ?
2. Can I read your newspaper ?
3. Can I take your dog for a walk ?
4. Can I clean the car ?
5. Can I go to the cinema ?

5 **What time is it?**

1. It's size o'clock.
2. It's three o'clock.
3. It's seven o'clock.
4. It's five o'clock.
5. It's ten o'clock.
6. It's troo o'clock.
7. It's eleven o'clock.
8. It's nine o'clock.

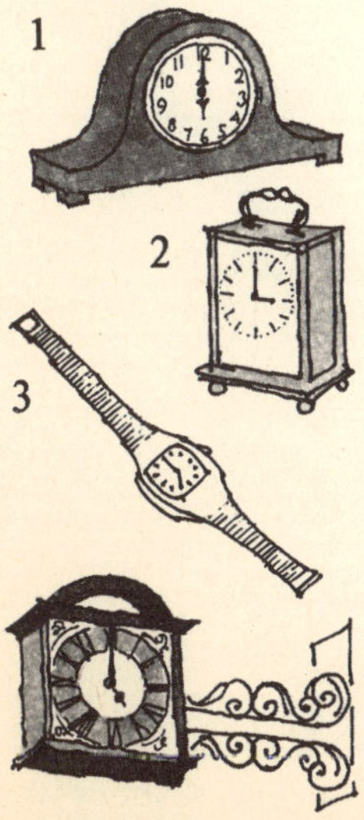

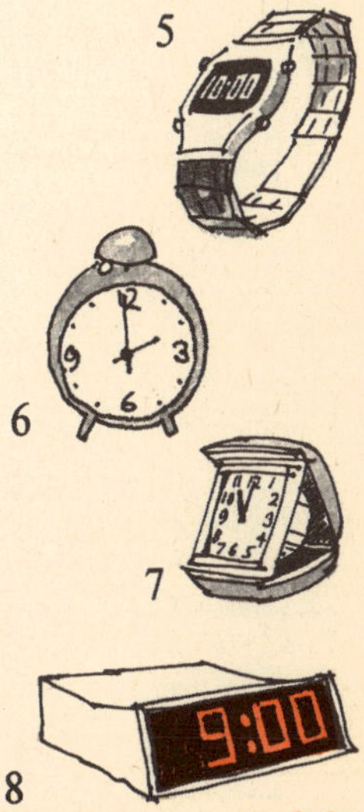

6 What can Peter do at the youth club?

watch　ride　buy　play　read

1. He ___can play___ in the garden.
2. He can watch TV.
3. He can ride his bike.
4. He can buy records.
5. He can read books.

7

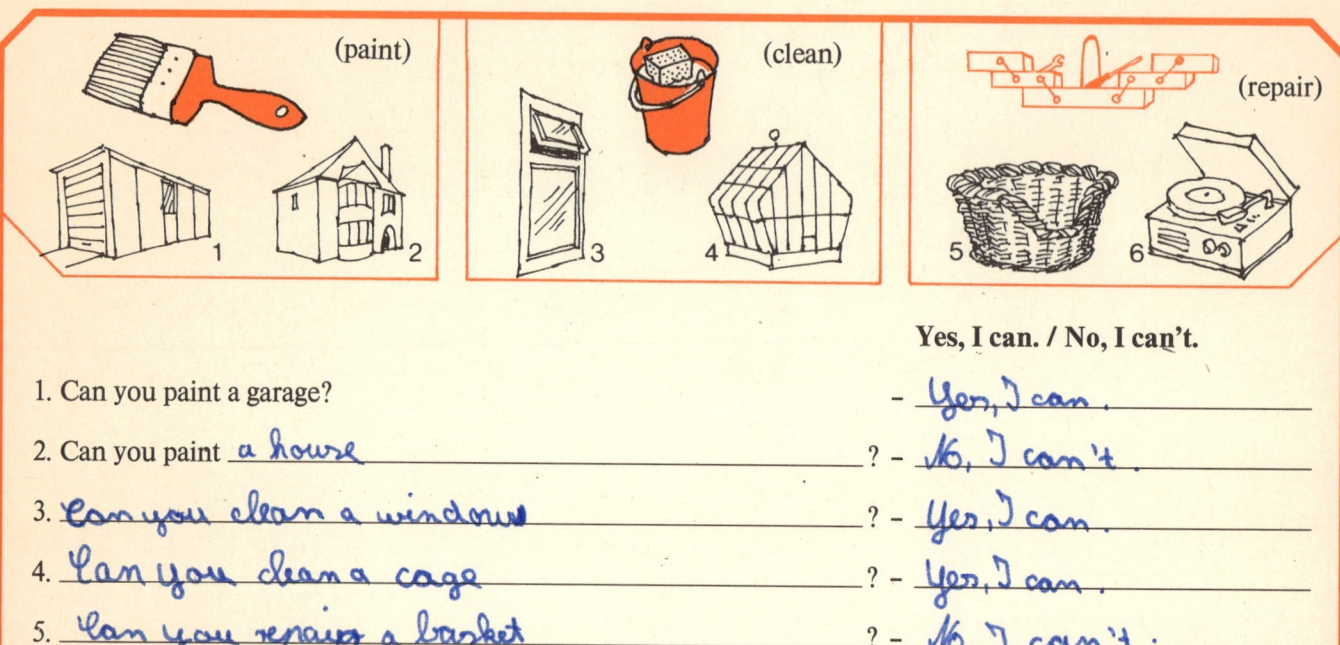

Yes, I can. / No, I can't.

1. Can you paint a garage? — Yes, I can.
2. Can you paint a house? — No, I can't.
3. Can you clean a window? — Yes, I can.
4. Can you clean a cage? — Yes, I can.
5. Can you repair a basket? — No, I can't.
6. Can you repair a record-player? — No, I can't.

8

1. Tony can't play with his friends.
2. Dave can't run after his dog.
3. Johnny can't carry the bag.
4. Ann can't go to school.
5. Peter can't read the poster.

9a Pupils at King School and their pets.

What have they got?

1. John Abel has got a hamster.
2. Phil and Jane Edwards have got a dog.
3. Sally Drew hasn't got a pet.
4. Peter Green has got two cats.
5. Frank and John Hill has got a cat and a budgie.
6. Mary Fox has got three rabbits.
7. Jim and Linda Long haven't got a pet.
8. Mike Jones has got a rabbit and a hamster.
9. Jill Brown has got a dog and a budgie.

And you?

I haven't got a pet.

9b
1. His name is Mike Jones. He's in Class 5A. He has got a rabbit and a hamster.
2. Her name is Jill Brown. She's in class 2B. She has got a dog and a budgie.
3. Their names are Frank and John Hill. They're in class 2F and 4A. They've got a cat and a budgie.
4. His name is John Abel. He's in class 1E. He has got a hamster.
5. Her name is Mary Fox. She's in class 3C. She has got three rabbits.
6. Their names are Phil and Jane Edwards. They're in class 2A and 4A. They've got a dog.
7. His name is Peter Green. He's in class 1D. He has got two cats.

10

1 — a box
2 — a cage
3 — a window
4 — a basket
5 — a goldfish
6 — a mouse

11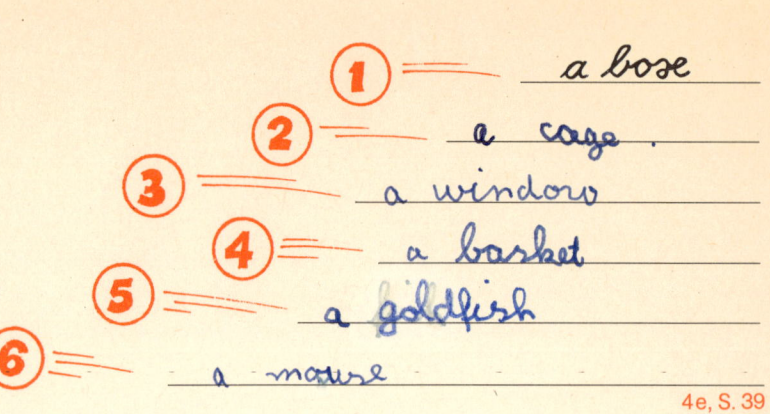

| A1 | B2 | C3 | D4 | E5 | F6 | G7 | H8 | I9 | J10 | K11 | L12 | M13 |

Paul: 9' 22 5   7 15 20   1   13 15 21 19 5   9 14   13 25   2 1 7.

I've got a Mouse in my bag.

Mike: 20 5 18 18 9 6 9 3 !   9 20   3 1 14   18 21 14
      1 6 20 5 18   20 8 5   7 9 18 12 19.

Terrific! It can run after the girls.

| N14 | O15 | P16 | Q17 | R18 | S19 | T20 | U21 | V22 | W23 | X24 | Y25 | Z26 |

12 Judy: Hallo, Chris. *Can you come to my house*? | come/my/to/house/you/Can |

Chris: Sorry, I can't. *I'm painting the balcony.* | the/painting/balcony/I'm |

Judy: Hm... *Can I come to your house*? | I/house/to/come/Can/your |

Chris: Yes. *You can clean the windows.* | can/windows/the/clean/You |

Judy: Oh! *It's raining now.* | now/raining/It's |

Chris: All right. *We can go to the cinema.* | We/cinema/to/go/can/the |

Judy: OK, Chris. Goodbye.   Chris: Bye, Judy.

13 What's in the cage?

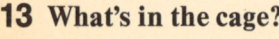
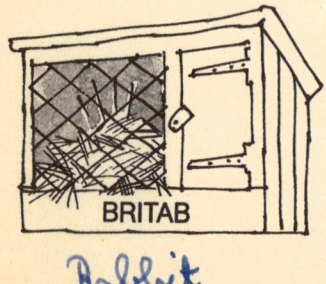
BRITAB — Rabbit

EIDBUG — budgie

SOEMU — Mouse

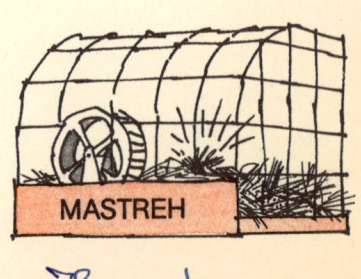
MASTREH — Hamster

Unit 5

1a Have you got to help at home?

	Ann:	Tom:
1. Have you got to clean your room?	Yes, I have.	No, I haven't.
2. Have you got to wash the dishes?	No, I haven't.	Yes, I have.
3. Have you got to go to the shops?	No, I haven't.	Yes, I have.
4. Have you got to help in the kitchen?	Yes, I have.	No, I haven't.
5. Have you got to make your bed?	Yes, I have.	Yes, I have.

5a, S. 41

1b

1. Ann **has got to** clean her room.
2. She **hasn't got to** wash the dishes.
3. She hasn't got to go to the shops.
4. She has got to help in the kitchen.
5. She has got to make her bed.

6. Tom **hasn't got to** clean his room.
7. He **has got to** wash the dishes.
8. He hasn't got to go to the shops.
9. He hasn't to got to help in the kitchen.
10. He has got to make my bed.

I've got to / I haven't got to

I've got to clean my room. clean my room.
I haven't got to wash the dishes.
I haven't got to go to the shops.
I've got to help in the kitchen.
I've got to make my bed.

5a, S. 41

2a

What have they got to do on Saturday?

1. Steve **has got to** repair his bike.
2. Sally and Jill **have got to** help in the kitchen.
3. Mary has got to clean her room.
4. John and Kate have got to paint the garage.
5. Paul has got to go to the shops.
6. Bill and Peter have got to wash the car.

5a, S. 42

2b Saturday

1.
Tom: Can you come to the youth club?
Steve: Not now. I've got to repair my bike.

2.
Pam: Can you come to the zoo?
Sally and Jill: Not now. We've got to help in the kitchen.

3.
Bob: Can you come to the cinema?
Mary: Not now. I've got to clean my room.

4.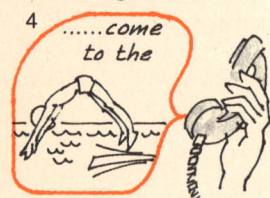
Jane: Can you come to the baths?
John and Kate: Not now. We've got to paint the garage.

5.
Linda: Can you come to the library?
Paul: Not now. I've got to go to the shops.

6.
Ted: Can you come to the youth club?
Bill and Peter: Not now. We've got to wash the car.

5a, S. 42

3

Mr Lee: Can I help you?
Jim: Yes, please. I'd like two bottles of lemonade.
Mr Lee: Anything else?
Jim: Yes. I'd like a packet of crisps, too.
Mr Lee: Here you are.
Jim: Thank you.

Miss Dunn: Can I help you?
Tony: Yes, please. I'd like a paint-brush.
Miss Dunn: Anything else?
Tony: Yes. I'd like a litre of white paint, too.
Miss Dunn: Here you are.
Tony: Thank you.

Mr Baker: Can I help you?
Doris: Yes, please. I'd like some cakes.
Mr Baker: Anything else?
Doris: Yes, I'd like some biscuits, too.
Mr Baker: Here you are.
Doris: Thank you.

Mrs Tay: Can I help you?
Pam: Yes, please. I'd like a bottle of milk.
Mrs Tay: Anything else?
Pam: Yes, I'd like a bottle of lemonade, too.
Mrs Tay: Here you are.   Pam: Thank you.

Mr Dee: Can I help you?
Janet: Yes, please. I'd like a magazine.
Mr Dee: Anything else?
Janet: Yes, I'd like a newspaper, too.
Mr Dee: Here you are.   Janet: Thank you.

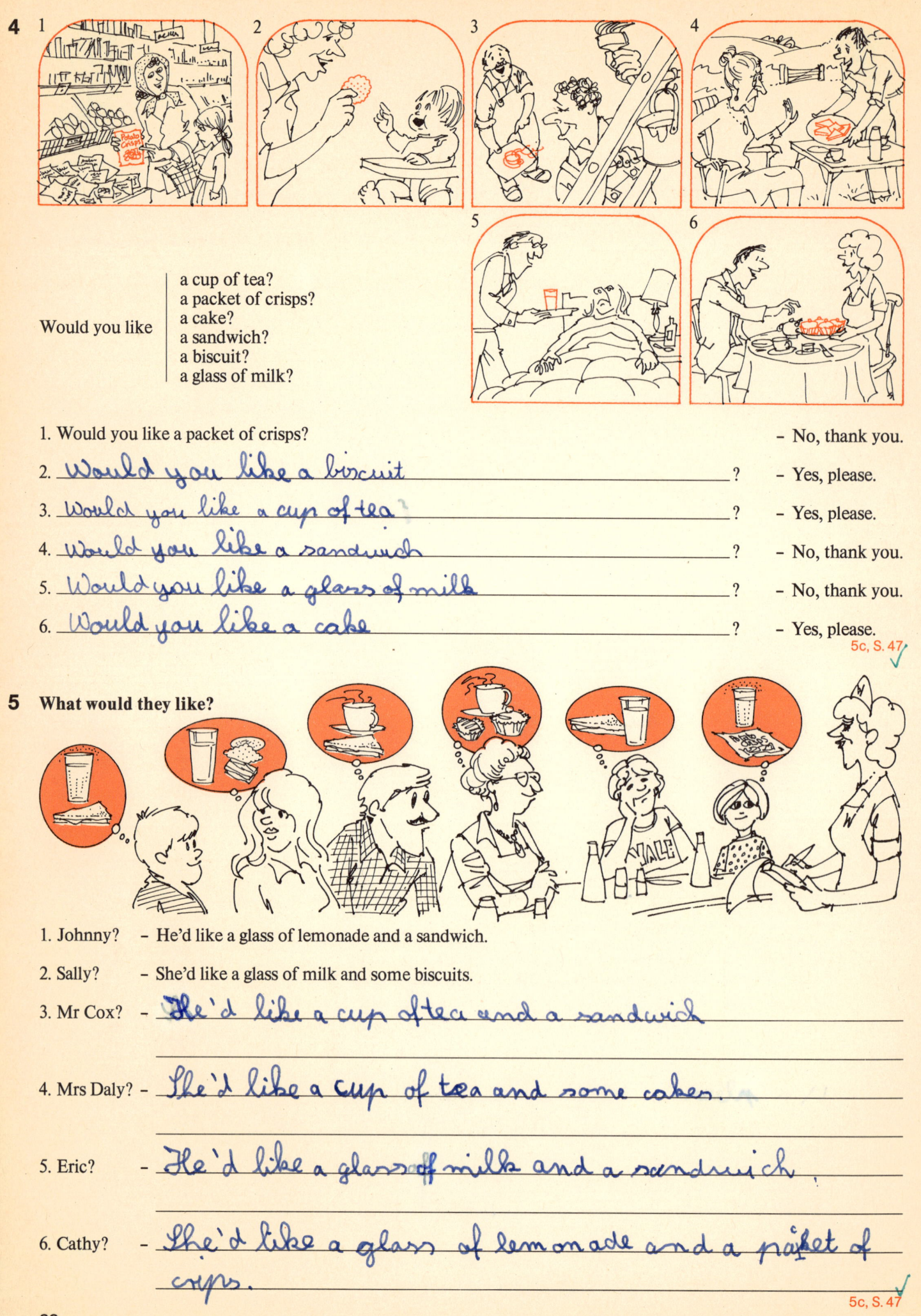

6

I'd like a big room. I'd like a brown door and a white ceiling. I'd like a red walls, too.

Daniela Pfeiffer

7a

1. Four litres of yellow paint.
2. Two litres of white paint.
3. One litre of red paint
4. Six litres of brown paint.
5. One litre of blue paint.
6. Five litres of black paint

7b

1 = YELLOW
2 = WHITE
3 = RED
4 = GREEN
5 = BLUE
6 = BROWN

Mrs Trend:

Paint the walls _green_ and _white_, please.
Paint the ceiling _blue_ and _white_, please.
Paint the doors _brown_ and _red_, please.
Paint the windows _brown_ and _yellow_, please.

Unit 6

1
1. *Pam:* I collect models.
2. *Jill:* I collect _stamps._
3. *Bob:* _I collect coins._
4. *Tom:* _I collect magazines._
5. *Sue:* _I collect records._
6. *Bill:* _I collect casettes._

6a, S. 52

2
1. Pam and Bill _go to_  the youth club every Tuesday.
2. Bob and Jim _go to_  the baths every Wednesday.
3. Sue and Rita _go to_  the cinema every Saturday.
4. Mary and Tom _go to_  the library every Friday.

6a, S. 52

3

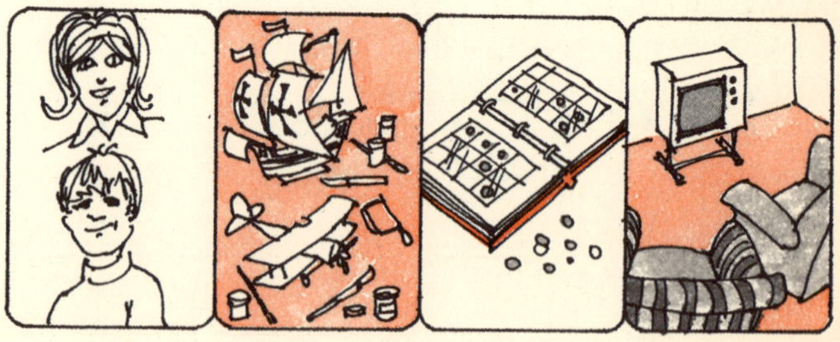

Jim and Sue	work play read	in a shop.	☒ ☐ ☐	Sally and Dave	make ride take	models.	☒ ☐ ☐
They	learn repair watch	lots of bikes.	☐ ☒ ☐	They	read meet ask	in the model club.	☐ ☒ ☐
They	learn collect talk	judo every Tuesday.	☒ ☐ ☐	They	collect run after play	coins, too.	☒ ☐ ☐
They	go play wash	table-tennis, too.	☐ ☒ ☐	They	ride make watch	TV every evening.	☐ ☐ ☒

6b, S. 53

24

4 Hobbies

1. *Sue and Rod:* We take photos and we collect stamps.
2. *Doris:* I play table-tennis and I make models.
3. *Mike:* I play table-tennis and I collect stamps.
4. *Jim and Tom:* We learn judo and we make models.
5. *Jenny:* I learn judo and I collect stamps.
6. *Peter:* I take photos and I make models.
7. *Ann and Jane:* We play table-tennis and we play football.
8. *David:* I take photos and I play football.
9. *Mary:* I learn judo and I play football.

And you? I play tennis and I collect stamps.

5 What's your dad's job? – works

1. *Dave:* He works in an office.
2. *Mary:* He works in a shop.
3. *Carol:* He works in a library.
4. *Kevin:* He works in a cinema.
5. *Susan:* He works in a school.

6 What's your mum's job? – does – makes – paints – repairs – sells

1. *Dave:* She does the housework.
2. *Mary:* She sells cakes.
3. *Carol:* She repairs TVs.
4. *Kevin:* She paints bikes.
5. *Susan:* She makes baskets.

7 German or English?

1. An English policeman.
2. A German newspaper.
3. An English car.
4. An English newspaper.
5. A German car.
6. A German magazine.
7. A German policeman.
8. An English magazine. ✓

8

1. The number four bus goes to _____ Sutton.
   It leaves at half past eight.
   It arrives at nine o'clock.

2. The number nine bus goes to _____ Dorking.
   It leaves at quater past eight.
   It arrives at quater to nine.

3. The number eight bus goes to _____ Epsom.
   It leaves at eight o'clock.
   It arrives at half past nine.

6c, S. 55

9 The Whites

1. Mr White leaves home at half past seven.
   He starts work at nine o'clock.
   He finishes work at five o'clock.
   He arrives home at half past six.

2. Mrs White leaves home at half past eight.
   She starts work at quater past nine.
   She finishes work at quater past nine.
   She arrives home at quater past one.

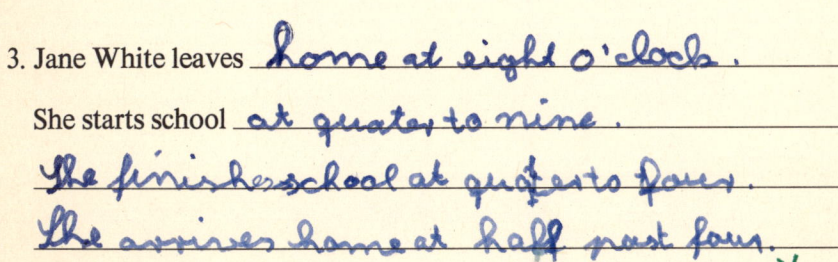

3. Jane White leaves home at eight o'clock.
   She starts school at quater to nine.
   She finishes school at quater to four.
   She arrives home at half past four.

4. David White leaves home at quater to nine.
   He starts school at quater past nine.
   He finishes school at quarter past three.
   He arrives home at quater to four.

6c, S. 55

10

	1	2	3	4	5	6	7	8
Monday	✓			✓				✓
Tuesday	✓		✓	✓				✓
Wednesday	✓			✓				✓
Thursday	✓			✓		✓		✓
Friday	✓			✓			✓	✓
Saturday		✓		✓				✓
Sunday		✓		✓	✓			✓

goes (3 x) – works (2 x) – watches – plays – rides

1. Dave Swift works in an office.
2. He _works in the garden_ at the weekend.
3. He _goes to the library_ on Tuesday.
4. He _watches TV_ every day.
5. He _plays football_ on Sunday.
6. He _goes to the photo club._ on Thursday.
7. He _goes to the shops_ on Friday.
8. He _rides his bike_ every day.

6c, S. 55 ✓

11 at (2 x) – in (4 x) – on (2 x) – to – with (2 x)

My dad leaves home _at_ seven o'clock _in_ the morning. He works _in_ an office. He arrives home _at_ five o'clock. He helps me _with_ my homework _in_ the evening. He goes _to_ the shops _with_ my mum _on_ Saturday. We play football _in_ the park _at_ Sunday morning. My dad is very nice.

6e, S. 58

12

1. Coins
2. Table-tennis
3. Planes
4. Stamps
5. Football
6. Photos
7. Models

6e, S. 58 ✓

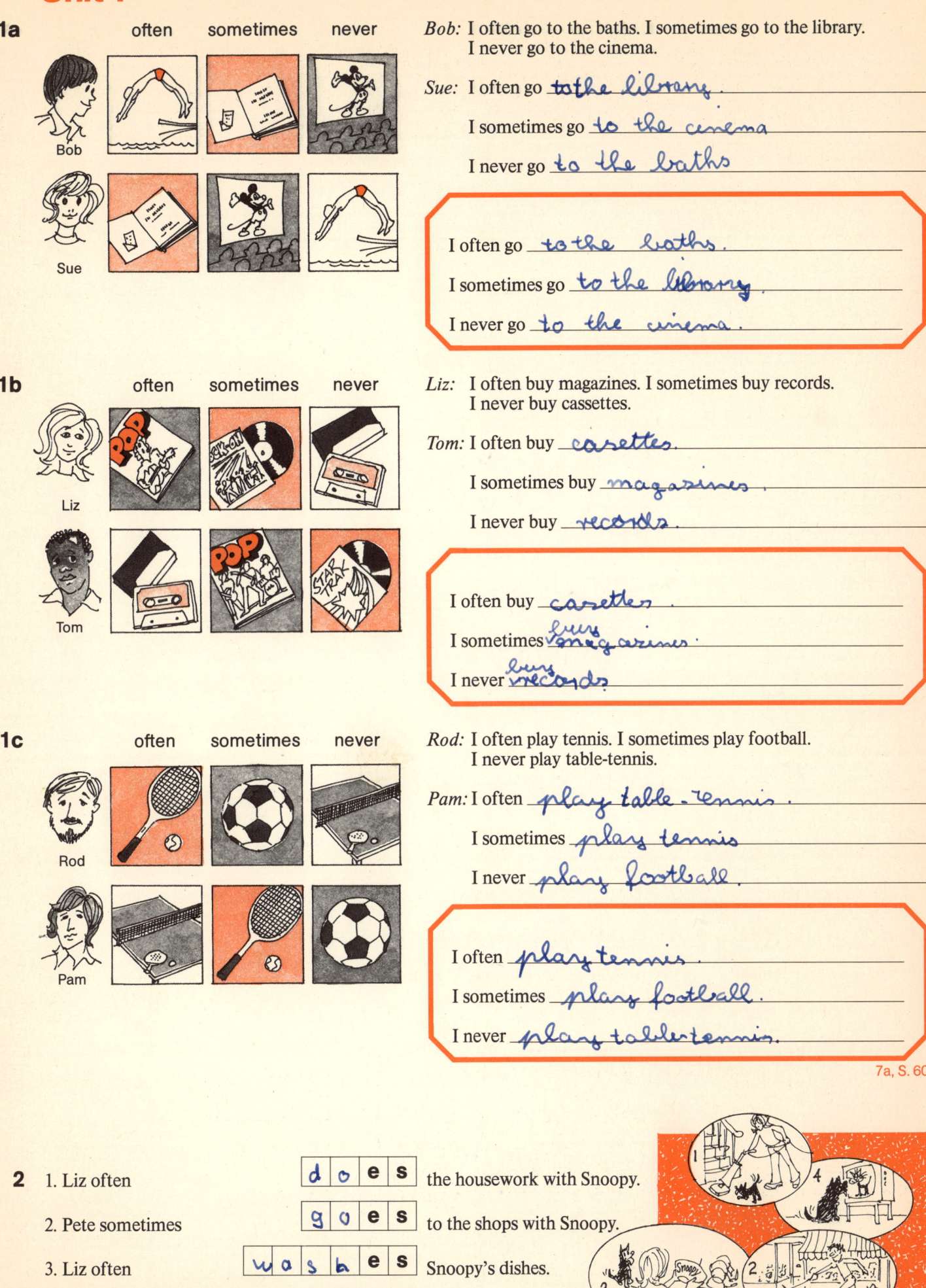

3 Mr West works in an office. Mrs West sells books. Mike West repairs cars. Helen West goes to school. Woofie plays in the garden.

But the Wests are on holiday now.

Mr West is lying on the beach.
Mrs West is reading a book on the beach.
Mike is playing football on the beach.
Helen is swimming in the sea.
Woofie is lying on the beach.

1. Mr West works in an office.   He **isn't working** in the office now.

    He**'s lying** on the beach.

2. Mrs West sells books.   She _isn't selling books now._
She is reading a book on the beach.

3. Mike West repairs cars.   He _isn't repairing cars now._
He's playing football on the beach

4. Helen West goes to school.   She _isn't going to school now_
She's swimming in the sea

5. Woofie plays in the garden.   He _isn't playing in the garden now._
He's lying on the beach.

7b, S. 61

4

1. *Mr West:* Hotels are terrific because I haven't got to work in the garden.

2. *Helen West:* Hotels are terrific because I _haven't got to make the bed._

3. *Mike West:* _Hotels are terrific because I haven't to clean the room_

4. *Mrs West:* _Hotels are terrific because I haven't got to wash the dishes._

7b, S. 61

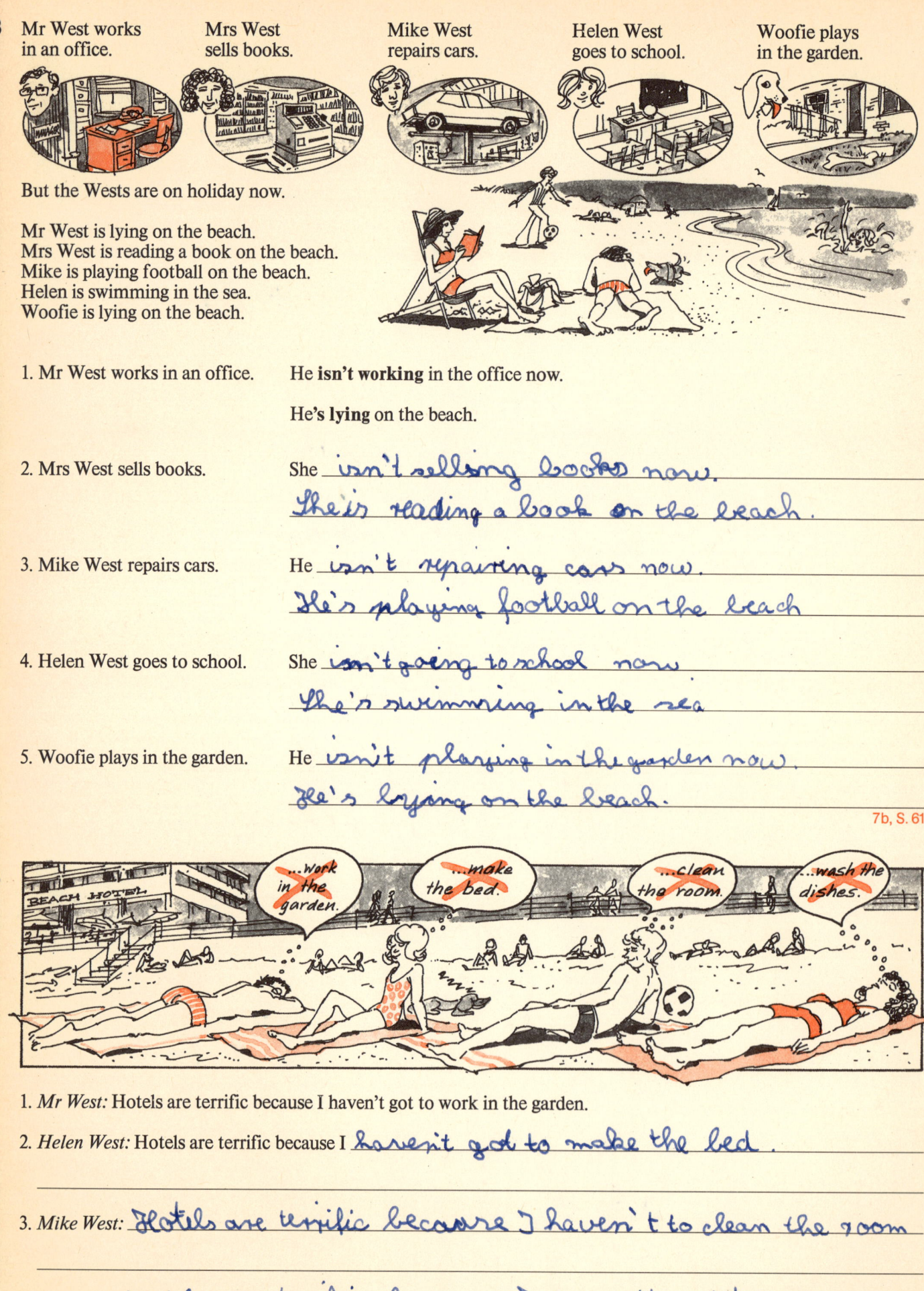

5a

1. Sue often goes on holiday in August.
   She stays at hotels.

2. Pia and Mario often go on holiday in May.
   They stay at camp sites.

3. Olaf often goes on holiday in June.
   He stays at youth hotels.

4. Sally and Mike often goe on holiday in April.
   They stay at a carvan sites.

5. Ina often goes on holiday in September.
   She stays at a youth hotels.

6. Marie and Pierre often goe on holiday in July.
   They stay at a carvan sites.

5b

OFTEN | THIS YEAR

1. *Sue:* I often go to Spain.
   But this year I'm going to Yugoslavia.

2. *Pia and Mario:* We often go to Austria.
   But this year we're going to Britain.

3. *Olaf:* I often goe to Yugoslavia.
   But this year I'm going to Italy.

4. *Sally and Mike:* We often goe to Denmark.
   But this year we're going to Austria.

5. *Ina:* I often go to Italy.
   But this year I'm going to Denmark.

6. *Marie and Pierre:* We often go to Britain.
   But this year we're going to Spain.

6

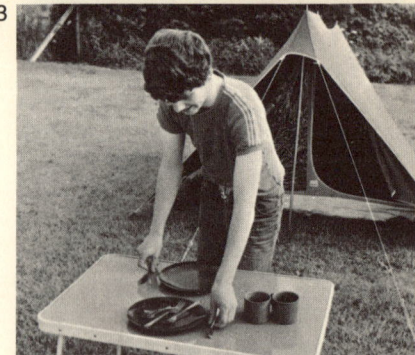
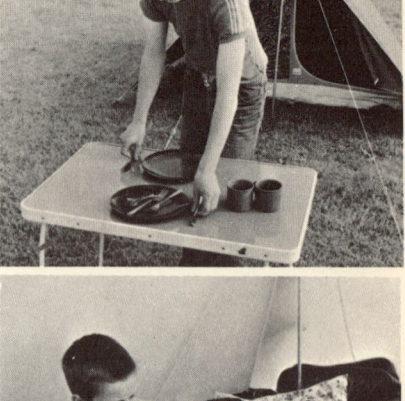

Carol: Here's Jack. He's drying the dishes.

Mum: He never dries the dishes at home.

1. *Carol:* Here's Tony. He's making a cup of tea.
   Mum: He never _makes a cup of tea_ at home.

2. *Carol:* Here's Jack. He's reading a book.
   Mum: He _never reads a book_ at home.

3. *Carol:* Here's Tony. He's laying the table.
   Mum: He _never lays the table at home_

4. *Carol:* Here's Jack. He's making his bed.
   Mum: He _never makes his bed at home_

Carol: But Mum, you've got lots of time on holiday.

7c, S. 63

7

Would you like a crisp? ⑤
Are you going to the beach, too? ④
Are you English? ②
Excuse me, how can I get to the beach? ①
Can you say that again, please? ⑤
Can we meet this evening? ⑦
Where are you staying? ③

8 at – in – on – to – with

It's raining here in Southend. We've staying at a hotel with TV in every room. We've going to the beach this afternoon. Rain or no rain. Can you come to our house at Wednesday next week?
Jim xx

Sue White,
19, Terrace Gdns,
Hatfield,
Hertfordshire.
England.

Dear Sue,
Here I am in Scotland. The sun is shining and I'm lying on the beach. I'm in holiday with my mum and dad and my brother. There's a nice German boy at the next caravan.
Love Jane xxx

Susan White,
19, Terrace Gdns.,
Hatfield – Herts.
England.

9 JANUARY – FEBRUARY – MARCH – APRIL – MAY – JUNE – JULY – AUGUST – SEPTEMBER – OCTOBER – NOVEMBER – DECEMBER – JANUARY – FEBRUARY – MARCH – APRIL – MAY – JUNE – JULY – AUGUST – SEPTEMBER – OCTOBER – NOVEMBER – DECEMBER – JANUARY – FEBRUARY – MARCH

Unit 8

1 What time is it?

1. 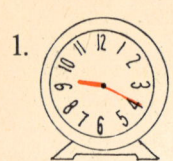 (9.20) It's twenty past nine.
2.  (11.10) It's ten past eleven.
3. 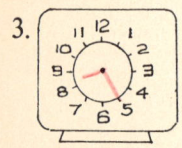 (8.25) It's twenty-five past eight.
4.  (2.15) It's quarter past two.
5. 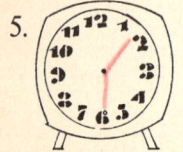 (1.30) It's half past one.
6. 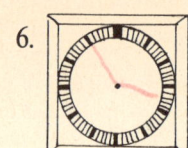 (3.55) It's five to four
7.  (6.40) It's twenty to seven
8.  (5.45) It's quarter to six.
9.  (7.35) It's twenty-five to eight.
10. 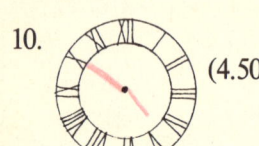 (4.50) It's ten to five

8a, S. 68

2

Let's buy a cassette.

Let's play table-tennis.

Let's meet at 6.00.

Let's go to the cinema

Let's watch The Pet"

Let's stay in a hotel

8a, S. 68

3 me – us

1. Can you help **me**?
2. Can you help **us**?
3. Can you help me?
4. Can you help me?
5. Can you help us?
6. Can you help us?

8a, S. 69

4 her – him – them

1. My mother often cleans the house. My father always helps _her_
2. My sisters often work in the garden. I never help _help_
3. Our friends often make cakes. We sometimes help _them_
4. My brother always clears the table. I often help _him_

8a, S. 69

5 me – him – her – us – them

1. Mum is going to the park. Are you going with _her_?
2. The boys are going to the cinema. Are you going with _them_?
3. Dad is going to the shops. Are you going with _him_?
4. I'm going to the model club. Are you going with _me_?
5. We're going to the zoo. Are you going with _us_?
6. The girls are going to the baths. Are you going with _them_?

8a, S. 70

6 you – him – her – us – them

1. *Bob:* Who's playing with Sue?
   Ted: Jane is _playing with her._

2. *Bob:* Who's playing with Sally and Jim?
   Ted: Mary and Mike are _playing with them_

3. *Bob:* Who's playing with you and me?
   Ted: _Dave and Mike are playing with us_

4. *Bob:* Who's playing with Mike?
   Ted: _Dave is playing with him._

5. *Bob:* Who's playing with me?
   Ted: _Jane is playing with you._

8a, S. 70

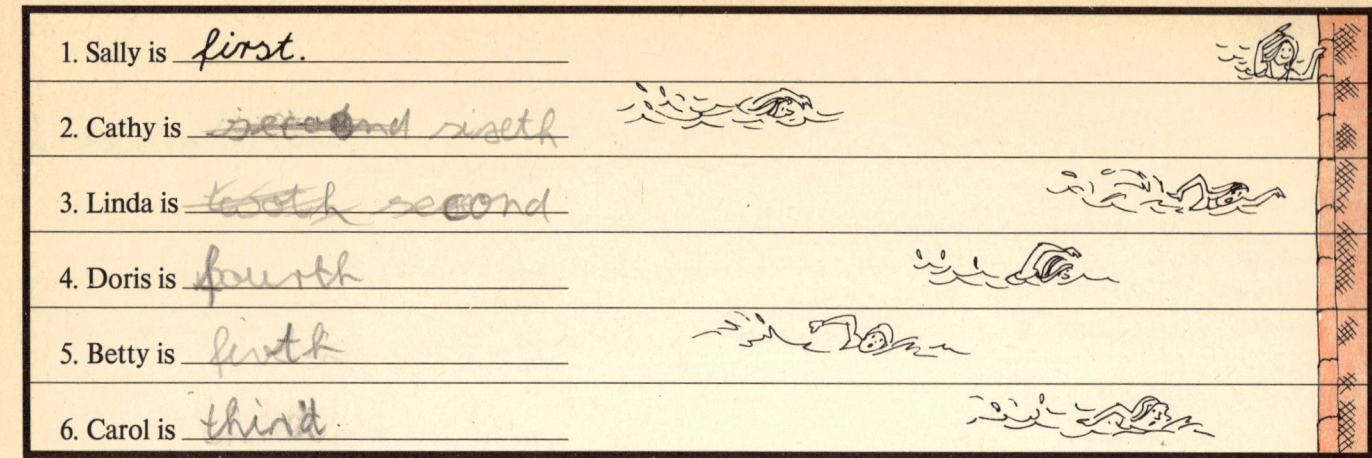

7
1. Sally is first.
2. Cathy is ~~second~~ sixth
3. Linda is ~~tenth~~ second
4. Doris is fourth
5. Betty is fifth
6. Carol is third

8 When are they going on holiday?

MAY				
Mon	5	12	19	26
Tues	6	13	20	27
Wed	7	14	21	28
Thurs	1	8	15	22	29
Fri	2	9	16	23	30
Sat	3	10	17	24	31
Sun	4	11	18	25

JUNE				
Mon	2	9	16	23	30
Tues	3	10	17	24
Wed	4	11	18	25
Thurs	5	12	19	26
Fri	6	13	20	27
Sat	7	14	21	28
Sun	1	8	15	22	29

JULY				
Mon	7	14	21	28
Tues	1	8	15	22	29
Wed	2	9	16	23	30
Thurs	3	10	17	24	31
Fri	4	11	18	25
Sat	5	12	19	26
Sun	6	13	20	27

AUGUST				
Mon	4	11	18	25
Tues	5	12	19	26
Wed	6	13	20	27
Thurs	7	14	21	28
Fri	1	8	15	22	29
Sat	2	9	16	23	30
Sun	3	10	17	24	31

Miss May is going on the second Saturday in May. That's May 10th.
Miss Grey is going on the fourth Sunday in August. That's August 24th.
Mrs Dale is going on the third Monday in July. Thats July 21th.
Mr Hill is going on the first Friday in July. Thats July 4th.
Mr Rice is going on the third Tuesday in June. Thats June 19th.
Dave Wood is going on the first Sunday in August. Thats August 3rd.

9 Birthdays

Mr Dale: 16. 12. 1944 — His birthday is on December 16th.
Mrs Dale: 3. 11. 1945 — Her birthday is on November 3rd
Susan Dale: 2. 2. 1978 — Her birthday is on February 2th.
Terry Dale: 24. 6. 1981 — His birthday is on June 24th.
Mr White: 1. 1. 1954 — His birthday is on January 1th.
Mrs White: 22. 7. 1957 — Her birthday is on July 22th.
Jim White: 23. 3. 1977 — His birthday is on March 23rd.
Mary White: 13. 5. 1979 — Her birthday is on May 13th.

And you? My birthday is on January 19

10

Your birthday	Yes, I would. / No, I wouldn't.
Would you like to have tea at home?	Yes, I would.
Would you like to go to the cinema?	No, I wouldn't.
Would you like to play records?	No, I wouldn't.
Would you like to watch TV?	No, I wouldn't.
Would you like to play games?	Yes, I would.
Would you like to dance?	No, I wouldn't.

8c, S. 73

11 Birthday presents

① Sue ② Tony ③ Mary ④ Mike ⑤ Carol ⑥ David

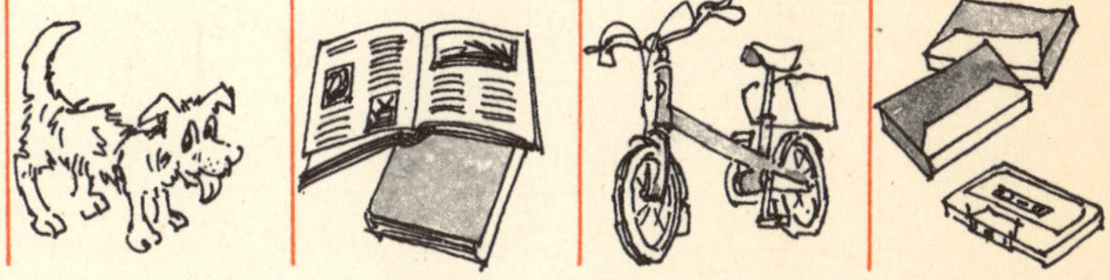

It's your birthday. What would you like to get?

1. *Sue:* **I'd like to get a** record-player.
2. *Tony:* **I'd like to get some** records.
3. *Mary:* I'd like to get a dog.
4. *Mike:* I'd like to get some books.
5. *Carol:* I'd like to get a bike.
6. *David:* I'd like to get some casettes.

8c, S. 74

12 A holiday in Scotland

EDINBURGH — Inverness — AVIEMORE — AYR — At home

Mum: I'd like to stay at a hotel in Edinburgh.

Tom: Oh no. Not Edinburgh. I'd like to stay at a hotel in Inverness.

Pam: Oh no. Not Inverness. I'd like to stay at a hotel in Aviemore.

Sue: Oh no. Not Aviemore. I'd like to stay at a hotel in Ayr.

Dad: Oh no. Not Ayr. I'd like to stay at home.

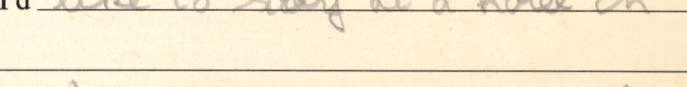

All: Oh no. Not at home!

8c, S. 74

Aviemore – [ævi'mɔː]   Ayr – [eə]   Inverness – [ɪnvə'nes]

13 Pam's birthday presents.

1. Lots of people can play with Mike's present.   It's a _play_
2. You can read Sally's present.   It's a _book_
3. Carol's present is in a box.   It's a _pencil_
4. Pete's present isn't in a box but it's expensive.   _It's a radio-recorder_
5. Dave's present is black.   _It's a record_
6. Pam can do her homework with Linda's present.   _It's a pen_

14

1. Would you like to dance?
2. Can I have the red paint, please?
3. How can I get to the zoo, please?
4. Would you like another cake?
5. What's that in English?
6. Let's go to the cinema.

A	B	C	D	E	F
6	1	5	3	2	4

15

ake + bony + cp + pane + fl + recd = ?

Jim's birthday present is a _calculator_

16 When is the first day of the holidays?

1. The first month.
2. The eighth month.
3. The fourth month.
4. The fifth month.
5. The second month.
6. The seventh month.
7. The ninth month.
8. The eleventh month.
9. The twelfth month.
10. The sixth month.
11. The tenth month.
12. The third month.

Crossword answer: JULY THE ELEVENTH

Unit 9

1

Dear Jane,
        Please can you go to the shops. Here's £1.50. Buy two litres of white paint.
                              Mum

Dear Carol,
        Please can you go to the shops. Here's 70p. Buy a bottle of ~~lemon~~ lemonade
                              Dave

Dear Mike,
        Please can you go to the shops. Here's 60p. Buy tea
                              Dad

Dear Bob,
        Please can you go to the shops. Here's 65p. Buy biscuits
                              Ted

Dear Dad,
        Please go to the shops. Here's £1.10. Buy three paint-brushes
                              Sally

Dear Mary,
        Please can you go to the shops. Here's £1.05. Buy cakes
                              Mum

2

1.	Carol:	**Yes, I do. / No, I don't.**	2.	John:	**Yes, I do. / No, I don't.**
Do you get pocket-money?		Yes, I do	Do you get pocket-money?		Yes, I do
Do you get £2 a week?		No, I don't	Do you get £1.50 a week?		No, I don't
Do you save?		Yes, I do	Do you save?		Yes, I do
Do you save 50p a week?		No, I don't	Do you save 75p a week?		No, I don't

And you?

Do you get pocket-money?   No, I don't   Do you save?   No, I don't

9a, S. 79

3 Every week

	Sally:	Tony: **Yes, I do. / No, I don't.**	You:
1.	Do you buy magazines?	Yes, I do.	Yes, I do
2.	Do you buy records?	No, I don't	No, I don't
3.	Do you buy sweets?	Yes, I do	Yes, I do
4.	Do you buy bus tickets?	No, I don't	No, I don't
5.	Do you buy posters?	No, I don't	No, I don't / Yes, I do
6.	Do you buy books?	Yes, I do	No, I don't
7.	Do you buy pens?	Yes, I do	Yes, I do
8.	Do you buy cinema tickets?	No, I don't	No, I don't

9b, S. 80

4 Ask a pop star

1. Do you collect records?
2. Do you play football?
3. Do you ride a bike?
4. Do you watch TV?
5. Do you get lots of money?
6. Do you meet lots of pop stars?
7. Do you go of tourne ?
8. Do you like the show- nousenis ?

5 Your friends

Do they | meet tea at your house?
| read you with your homework?
| help comics?
| learn you at the weekends?
| have TV every evening?
| watch English, too?

Yes, they do. / No, they don't.

1. Do they meet you at the weekends ?
2. ?
3. ?
4. ?
5. ?
6. ?

6 Your town

Do you like...?

Yes, I do. / No, I don't.

1. Do you like the shops ? Yes, I do
2. Do you like the baths ? Yes, I do
3. Do you like the parks ? No, I don't
4. Do you like the cinemas ? Yes, I do
5. Do you like the librarys ? Yes, I do

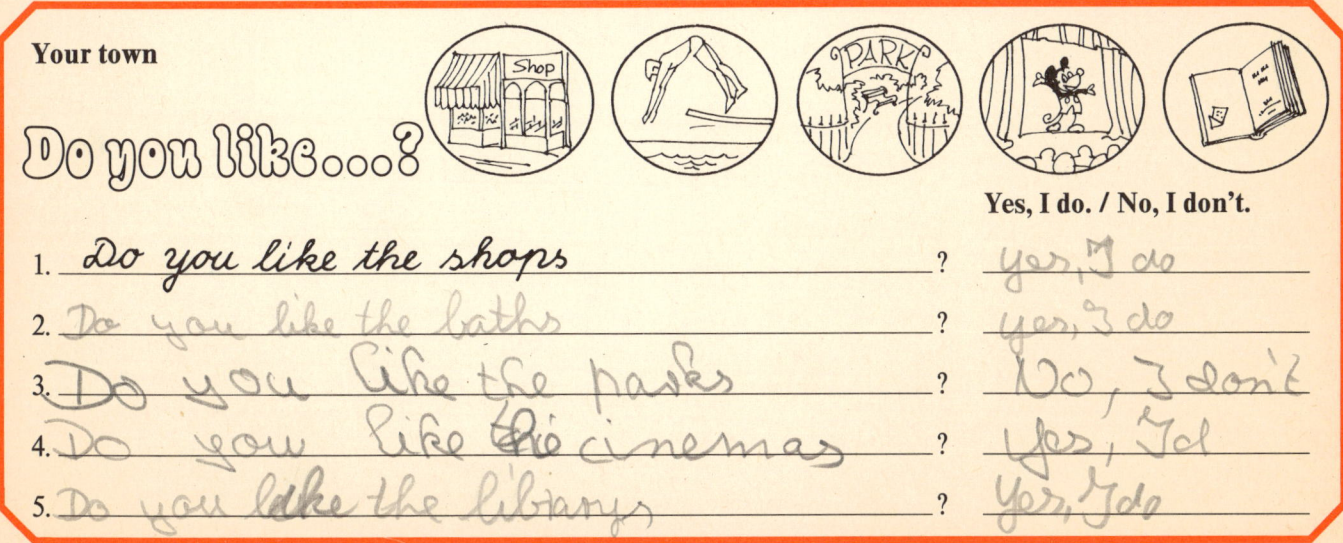

7

Do you go to the table-tennis club? — Yes, I do.
When do you meet? — We meet on Wednesday.
Where do you meet? — We meet in room 3.

Do _____ photo club? — Yes, I do.
When _____ ? — We meet on Friday.
Where _____ ? — We meet in room 10.

Do _____ ? — Yes, I do.
When _____ ? — We meet on Tuesday.
Where _____ ? — We meet in room 5.

_____ ? — Yes, I do.
_____ ? — We meet on Thursday.
_____ ? — We meet in room 8.

9b, S. 82

8

1. **What does the TV cost?** — £57
2. What does the _____ ? — _____
3. What _____ ? — _____
4. _____ ? — _____
5. _____ ? — _____

9c, S. 83

9

1. Does it play stereo music? — **Yes, it does.**
2. Does it work with batteries? — **No, it doesn't.**
3. Does it come with a case? — _____
4. Does it show the time? — _____
5. Does it play cassettes? — _____
6. Does it come with a headset? — _____
7. Does it play LPs? — *yes, it does*
8. Does it cost lots of money? — _____

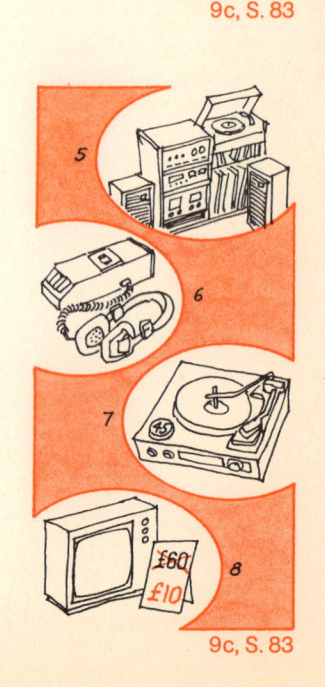

9c, S. 83

10 Alan's dog

Yes, it does. / No, it doesn't.

1. Does it like Alan? _____
2. Does it live in the house? _____
3. Does it watch TV? _____
4. Does it play with Alan? _____
5. Does it run after other pets? _____
6. Does it like cats? _____

11 do – does – don't – doesn't

1. _Does_ Jim like pop music? — Yes, he _does._
2. _____ Tom buy records? — No, he _____
3. _____ Pam and Jim like pop music? — Yes, they _____
4. _____ Pam buy cassettes? — No, she _____
5. _____ Jim and Pam like jazz? — No, they _____
6. _____ Tom like pop music? — _____
7. _____ Pam like folk music? — _____
8. _____ Jim and Pam buy cassettes? — _____
9. _____ Jim buy records? — _____
10. _____ Tom and Jim like folk music? — _____

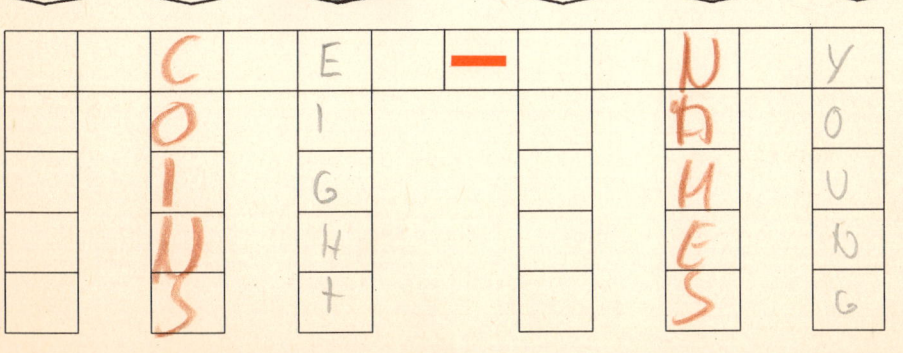

12

C O I N S   E I G H T   —   N A M E S   Y O U N G

Sally likes Fridays because she gets her _____

Unit 10

1

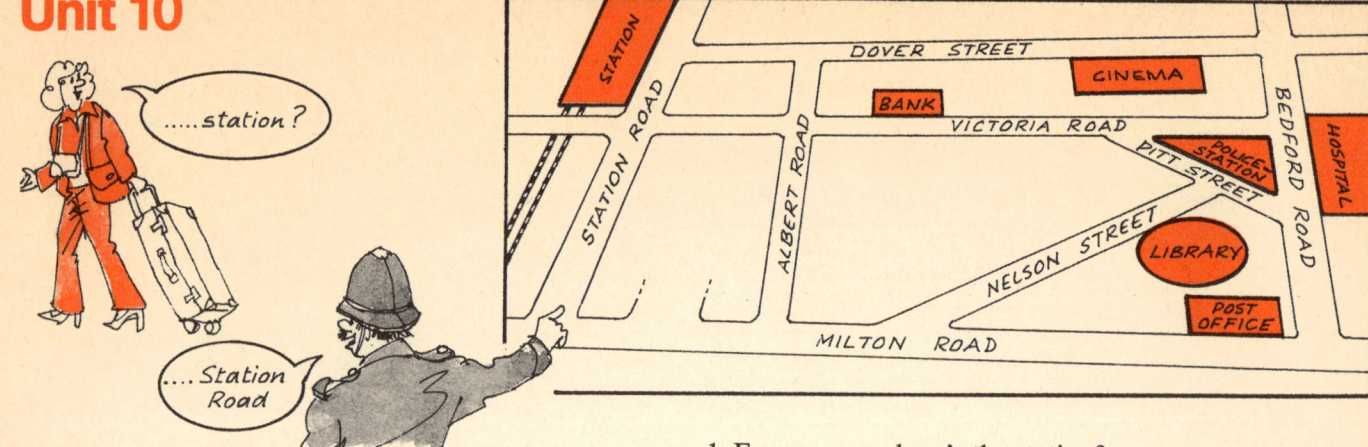

1. Excuse me, where's the station?
   – It's in Station Road.

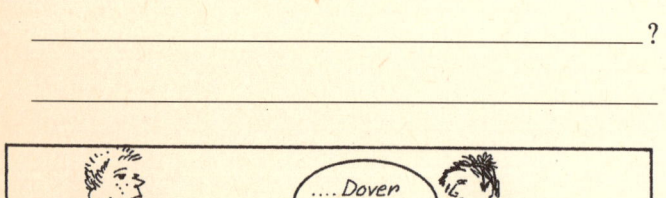

2. Excuse me, _____?
   – It's _____

3. _____?

4. _____?

5. _____?

6. _____?

7. _____?

2a on the left / on the right

1. Go along Bedford Road. Turn left into Dover Street.   The park _____
2. Go along Pitt Street. Turn left into Nelson Street.   The library _____
3. Go along Milton Road. Turn left into Albert Road.   The youth club _____
4. Go along Station Road. Turn right into Dover Street.   The baths _____

10a, S. 89

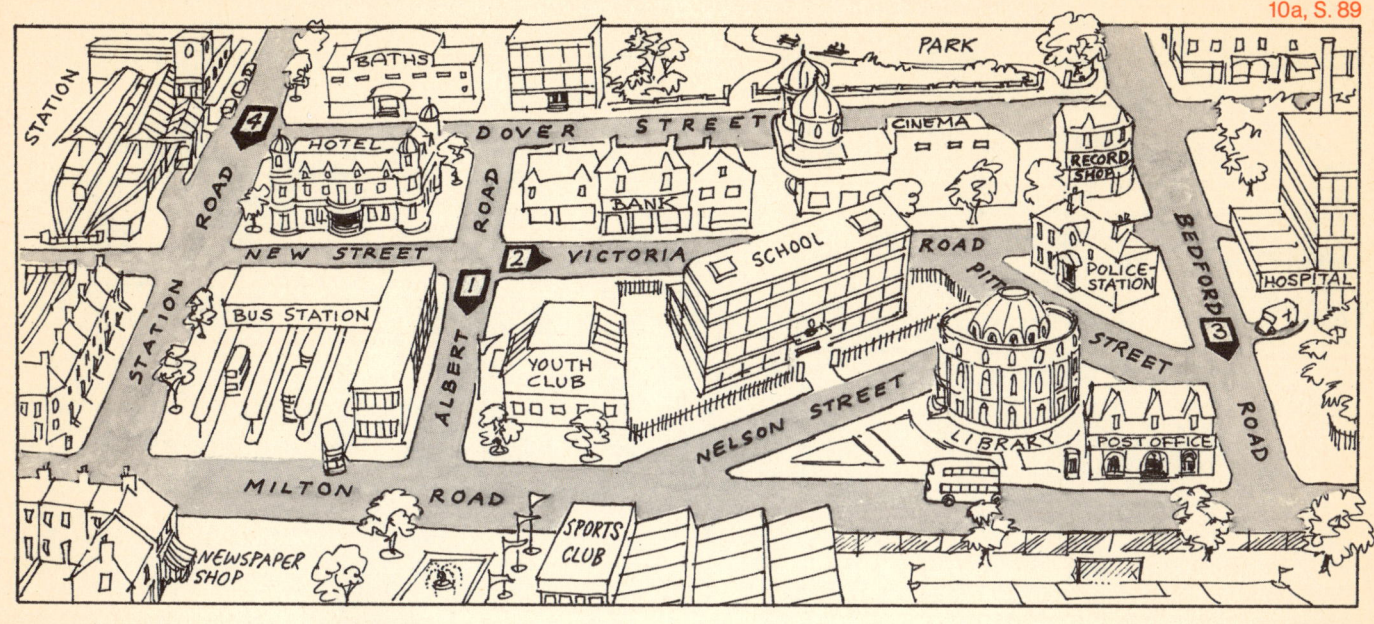

2b

1. Can you tell me the way to the newspaper shop, please?

   Go along Albert Road.

   Turn right into Milton Road.

   The newspaper shop **is on the left.**

2. Can you tell me the way to the record shop, please?

   Go _____
   Turn _____
   The record shop _____

3. Can you tell me the way to the sports club, please?

   Go _____
   Turn _____
   The _____

4. Can you tell me the way to the bus station, please?

   _____
   _____
   _____

10a, S. 89

3a Your town – Do you like the…?

	Yes	No		modern	old	small	big
baths	⊗	○		⊗	□	□	□
cinema	○	⊗		□	⊗	□	□
shops	⊗	○		□	□	□	⊗
library	⊗	○		⊗	□	□	□
schools	○	⊗		□	⊗	□	□
sports club	○	⊗		□	□	⊗	□

Martin:

I like the baths.

I don't like the cinema.

I _like the shops_

I _____

They're very modern.

It's very old.

They're _very modern_

It's _____

10b, S. 90

3b

Your town	I like / I don't like		modern / dirty / old / small / nice / terrible / big / terrific
baths	I like the baths	They're	terrific
cinema		It's	
shops	I ~~do~~ like the shops	They're	big
library	I like the library	It's	modern
schools			
sports club			

10b, S. 90

4

1. Ted **doesn't like** homework.
2. Pam _____
3. Dave _____
4. Jill _____
5. Mike _____

10b, S. 90

46

5a A school day

1. *Jack:* I go to school by bike.

    It takes twenty minutes.

    I have seven lessons every day.

    I eat at school.

    My homework takes half an hour.

2. *Carol:* I go _____

    It _____

    I have _____

    I eat at school _____

    My homework _____

3. *Mike:* I _____

    It _____

    I _____

    I _____

    My _____

    I _____
    It _____
    I _____
    I _____
    My _____

5b At the weekend

1. Jack **doesn't go** to school at the weekend.

    He **doesn't eat** at school at the weekend.

    He **doesn't do** homework at the weekend.

2. Carol _____ at the weekend.

    She _____ at the weekend.

    She _____ at the weekend.

3. Mike _____

    He _____

    He _____

6

Words in cloud: minute, crisps, sweets, sandwiches, day, police-station, bank, month, cake, post office, hotel, hour, biscuits, second, hospital

bank
post office
hotel
police-station
hospital

minute
hour, day
second, month

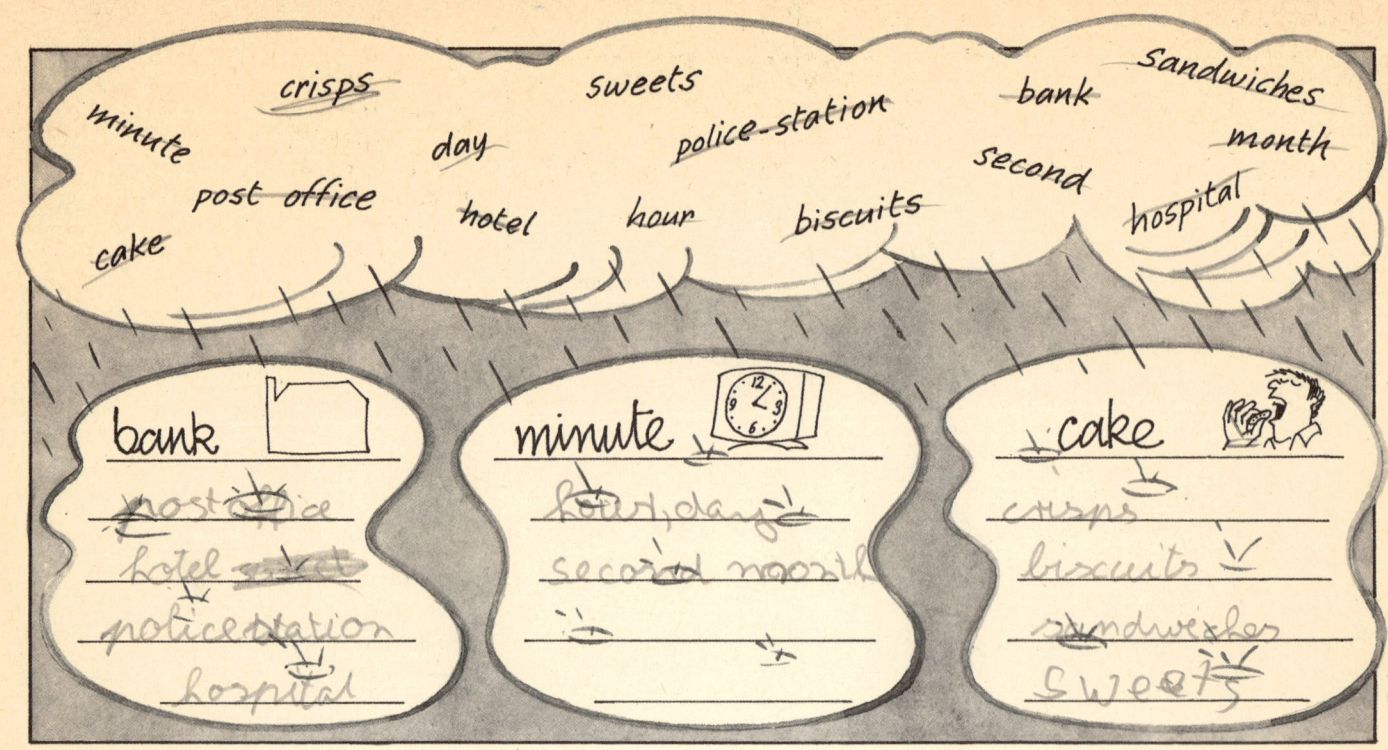

cake
crisps
biscuits
sandwiches
sweets

10e, S. 95

7 Yes or no?

		Yes		No	
1.	School often starts at nine o'clock in Britain.	Yes	Y O U	No	O Y U
2.	All English pupils wear school uniform.	Yes	E R N	No	R E N
3.	Some English pupils wear school uniform.	Yes	G L I	No	L I G
4.	Some English pupils eat sandwiches at school.	Yes	S H I	No	H I S
5.	English pupils go to school on Saturday.	Yes	V E S	No	S V E
6.	English pupils go home at one o'clock every day.	Yes	G R Y	No	R Y G
7.	English pupils go home at four o'clock every day.	Yes	O O D	No	O D O

| ¹ Y O U | ² E R N | ³ L I G | ⁴ H I S | ⁵ | ⁶ | ⁷ O D O |

10e, S. 95

Arbeitsheft zu ENGLISH H Neue Ausgabe · Band 1
Erarbeitet vom Cornelsen Verlag, Berlin
Verlagsredaktion:
Marie Keenoy (verantwortliche Redakteurin), Raymond Williams (Projektleitung)
Beratende Mitwirkung: Ingeborg Burgwitz, München; Prof. Harald Gutschow, Berlin; Prof. Dr. Peter W. Kahl, Hamburg; Prof. Hellmut Schwarz, Mannheim
Grafik: Roy Schofield, Cheam
Fotos: David Dore, Guildford, S. 1, S. 3; Peter de Kleine, Berlin, S. 3, S. 8, S. 33, S. 39; Klaus Wagner, Berlin, S. 1, S. 3, S. 8; J. Walmsley, Biggleswade, S. 6, S. 32

© 1982 Cornelsen Verlag GmbH & Co., Berlin
Das Werk und seine Teile sind urheberrechtlich geschützt. Jede Verwertung in anderen als den gesetzlich zugelassenen Fällen bedarf deshalb der vorherigen schriftlichen Einwilligung des Verlages.
Druck: Cornelsen Druck, Berlin
Schülerfassung: ISBN 3-464-04054-2 2. Auflage – 4. Druck 1988 Alle Drucke dieser Auflage können, weil untereinander unverändert, im Unterricht nebeneinander verwendet werden.

Vertrieb: Cornelsen Verlagsgesellschaft, Bielefeld